Cyberattack Shield: Protecting Your Home, Family, and Online Presence

A Practical Guide to Social Media Safety, Network Strengthening, and Surviving Digital Threats

Kylan P.crook

Copyright © 2024 by Kylan P.crook

All rights reserved. This book is an original work and copyrighted publication, protected under the laws of the United kingdom. No part of this book, including its content or any other material, may be reproduced or transmitted in any form or by any means, including photocopying, recording, or other electronic or mechanical methods without the prior written permission of the copyright owner. The information provided in this book is intended for personal use and educational purposes only.

Dedication

For those who seek to navigate the digital world safely, and for the families, friends, and colleagues we protect along the way. This book is dedicated to your vigilance, resilience, and commitment to a secure future.

Acknowledgment

My heartfelt thanks to everyone who contributed to this journey. To my family and friends, for their unwavering support and encouragement. To the cybersecurity professionals and communities whose insights and dedication continue to inspire and educate. And to the readers, for taking steps to secure their digital lives—this book is for you.

TABLE OF CONTENT

Dedication...2
Acknowledgment.................................... 3
Introduction.. 6
Chapter 1: The Basics of Cybersecurity and Common Cyber Threats..................... 13
Chapter 2: Building Cybersecurity Foundations at Home...22
Chapter 3: Strengthening Social Media Security. 31
Chapter 4: Safeguarding Children Online........ 40
Chapter 5: Protecting Vulnerable Family Members... 49
Chapter 6: Preparing for a Cyberattack........... 58
Chapter 7: Responding to Specific Cyberattacks 67
Chapter 8: Recovery and Rebuilding After an Attack...77
Chapter 9: Developing a Long-Term Cybersecurity Plan... 87
Chapter 10: Staying Updated on Cybersecurity Trends and Threats.......................97
Appendices and Resources...........................107
Conclusion...119

Introduction

In today's world, where technology touches almost every part of our lives, staying connected offers convenience and efficiency. However, alongside these benefits, digital spaces have become increasingly vulnerable to a host of cyber threats that range from phishing scams to sophisticated malware attacks. What was once limited to major corporations and government entities is now an everyday concern for individuals and small businesses alike. Cybercriminals are constantly evolving, adapting their tactics to exploit the most unsuspecting targets, often focusing on those who are less prepared for an attack. This shifting landscape of digital threats poses unique challenges that require everyone—not just tech experts—to be aware, vigilant, and ready.

For individuals, the impact of a cyberattack can be devastating and immediate. Imagine waking up to discover that your bank account has been drained or your personal data has been stolen. From identity theft to privacy breaches, cyberattacks can disrupt our lives in ways that go beyond the screen. Small businesses are similarly at risk, but they face the added difficulty of limited resources and smaller cybersecurity budgets compared to larger organizations. For many of these businesses, even a minor breach can be costly, not only financially but also in terms of reputation and customer trust. Small businesses are often targeted because attackers assume they lack sophisticated defenses, making them an appealing entry point for cybercriminals.

The most common types of cyber threats affecting both individuals and small businesses today include phishing, malware, ransomware, and data breaches. Phishing attacks, for example, often come through emails or messages designed to appear as if they're from trusted sources, tricking victims into providing sensitive information. Malware, or malicious software, is used to gain unauthorized access to systems, often causing harm to files and allowing hackers to spy on user activities. Ransomware goes a step further, encrypting data and holding it hostage until a ransom is paid. These threats are not just statistics; they represent real attacks affecting people and businesses every day, with significant consequences for anyone caught off guard.

In this environment of persistent threats, it's easy to feel overwhelmed. However, there's good news: proactive measures can significantly reduce the likelihood of falling victim to cyberattacks. This is where the concept of cyber resilience comes into play. Cyber resilience isn't just about preventing attacks; it's about building an ability to recover quickly and minimize damage when attacks do happen. Think of it as developing a digital immune system. By strengthening defenses and having a plan in place, you can create a safety net that allows you to respond effectively in the event of a breach, helping you to contain any potential fallout.

For individuals, cyber resilience means taking charge of one's digital life—knowing how to protect personal information, managing passwords wisely, and being mindful of the devices and networks used daily. For small businesses, cyber resilience can be the difference between survival and closure after a significant attack. Proactive digital security measures, such as regular data backups, employee training, and secure system configurations, can create a protective barrier against many threats. These steps aren't just about adding another layer of complexity; they're about creating peace of mind and establishing trust with clients and customers. A business that prioritizes cybersecurity demonstrates a commitment to protecting its clients' data, an invaluable asset in today's competitive marketplace.

This guide aims to serve as a practical resource for both individuals and small business owners seeking to strengthen their cybersecurity practices. We understand that not everyone has a technical background, and that's okay. This guide is crafted to make cybersecurity accessible and actionable, breaking down complex topics into clear steps that anyone can follow. From understanding common cyber threats to learning how to secure your social media accounts and home network, each chapter is designed to build your digital defenses, step-by-step. By the end of this book, you'll be equipped with the knowledge and tools necessary to not only prevent cyberattacks but also to respond confidently if one occurs.

One of the key goals of this guide is to shift the mindset around cybersecurity from reactive to proactive. Too often, people think about digital security only after an incident has happened. Our hope is to change that by emphasizing that cybersecurity doesn't have to be a burdensome task. It can be simple, effective, and, most importantly, empowering. The more you know about the digital threats you face, the better you can protect yourself, your family, and your business. In essence, cybersecurity is about taking ownership of your digital environment, treating it with the same care you would for your physical safety.

As you move through the pages of this guide, remember that building cyber resilience is an ongoing journey. Cyber threats evolve, and so should our defenses. Staying informed and prepared means regularly updating your knowledge and security practices, much like keeping up with health check-ups or car maintenance. The digital world may seem complex, but with the right approach, protecting yourself doesn't have to be.

This guide is more than a handbook; it's a companion for navigating the digital world safely. Cyber threats aren't going away, but neither is our ability to adapt and protect ourselves. Whether you're looking to protect personal information, secure your family's online presence, or safeguard a small business from cyber risks, this book offers the foundational steps you need to take control and stay secure in a connected world. By the end of this journey, you'll have gained not only knowledge but also a sense of empowerment, knowing that you can actively guard against and respond to the ever-present risks of the digital age.

Chapter 1: The Basics of Cybersecurity and Common Cyber Threats

Understanding Cybersecurity is essential in a world where technology has become central to everyday life. Cybersecurity encompasses the practices, tools, and techniques designed to protect digital systems, networks, and sensitive data from unauthorized access, attacks, or damage. It's not just a technical matter; it's a safeguard for privacy, financial stability, and personal security. Today, the importance of cybersecurity extends beyond large corporations and tech-savvy individuals to everyone who connects to the internet or uses digital devices.

This widespread need arises from the fact that our personal, professional, and financial information often resides online, making it a potential target for cybercriminals.

For most individuals, cybersecurity is about protecting personal data, including things like passwords, bank details, medical records, and social media information. Identity theft is one common consequence of weak personal cybersecurity; it can lead to financial loss, damage to one's credit score, and a long process of recovery. On the other hand, for small businesses, cybersecurity is equally, if not more, crucial. A single cyberattack can disrupt operations, lead to loss of customer trust, and incur financial costs that can be challenging to recover from, especially with limited resources. Small businesses often become targets because attackers assume they lack sophisticated defenses, making them easier to exploit.

A key principle of cybersecurity is that it's not just about technology; it's also about behavior. Developing a cybersecurity-conscious mindset involves recognizing risks, taking proactive steps to minimize them, and understanding the value of digital assets. Just as we lock our doors at night and take steps to protect our physical belongings, we must also establish practices to secure our online presence.

This mindset includes everything from setting strong passwords and updating software regularly to avoiding suspicious links and backing up important data. Understanding the basic concepts of cybersecurity can help individuals and small businesses build resilience against digital threats and establish practices that make them less vulnerable to attacks.

Overview of Common Threats gives us a window into the tactics cybercriminals frequently use to exploit vulnerabilities. Cyber threats are constantly evolving, and attackers utilize various methods to gain unauthorized access or cause harm. The most commonly encountered types of cyber threats today include phishing, malware, ransomware, and data breaches. Each of these threats operates in distinct ways but ultimately aims to exploit weak points, whether they be technical, procedural, or human vulnerabilities. Recognizing these threats helps individuals and businesses take specific steps to safeguard themselves and reduce the chances of becoming a target.

Phishing and Social Engineering are among the most deceptive and effective tools in a cybercriminal's arsenal. Phishing is a tactic that tricks individuals into divulging sensitive information by posing as a trustworthy source. It often arrives via email or text message, disguised as a legitimate request from a reputable organization, such a bank or government agency. For example, a phishing email might ask you to click a link to reset your password, leading you to a fake website designed to capture your login credentials.

Social engineering is a broader term that encompasses any attempt to manipulate individuals into taking actions that compromise security. These tactics exploit human psychology, often appealing to emotions such as urgency, fear, or curiosity to prompt people to act without caution.

Phishing can take on many forms, including email phishing, voice phishing (or "vishing"), and SMS phishing (or "smishing"), each tailored to a specific medium. A particularly dangerous form of phishing, known as spear-phishing, is highly targeted and personalized, making it seem as though the message is from a trusted source. Attackers may use information gathered from social media profiles or public records to craft messages that appear authentic. The best defense against phishing and social engineering is skepticism.

Always verify unexpected requests, avoid clicking unknown links, and think twice before providing sensitive information. By fostering this caution, individuals and businesses can build a stronger defense against these manipulative tactics.

Malware and Ransomware are other prevalent forms of cyber threats that target both individuals and businesses. Malware, short for "malicious software," is any software designed to cause harm to a system, whether by stealing data, spying on activities, or damaging files. Malware comes in various forms, including viruses, worms, spyware, and trojans. Viruses are programs that attach themselves to legitimate files and spread when these files are shared, while worms replicate independently and spread across networks. Spyware is designed to secretly monitor user activity and steal information, while trojans disguise themselves as harmless programs, unleashing malicious actions once installed.

Ransomware is a particularly destructive form of malware that encrypts a victim's files and demands payment, often in cryptocurrency, to unlock them.

Victims are essentially locked out of their own data, with a ransom demand as the only means to regain access.

However, paying the ransom does not guarantee the return of the data and may even encourage attackers to target other individuals or businesses. To combat malware and ransomware, regular data backups, updated antivirus software, and avoiding suspicious downloads are essential defenses. These practices can help minimize the impact of an attack and reduce the likelihood of infection.

Data Breaches and Insider Threats pose unique challenges, especially for organizations. A data breach occurs when sensitive information is accessed, stolen, or exposed without authorization. Breaches can result from weak passwords, outdated software, or sophisticated hacking techniques that target vulnerabilities in systems. The fallout from a data breach can be extensive, affecting everything from personal finances to a company's reputation. For individuals, compromised data may lead to identity theft or fraud, while for businesses, it can mean legal repercussions, financial loss, and loss of customer trust.

Insider threats, meanwhile, are risks that originate within an organization. These threats can come from employees, contractors, or even former staff members who have access to sensitive information. Insider threats may be unintentional, resulting from negligence or lack of awareness, or they may be malicious, with individuals intentionally misusing their access for personal gain or revenge. Insider threats are particularly challenging to detect because the people involved have legitimate access to the data they compromise.

Addressing insider threats requires a balanced approach, such as limiting access to sensitive information, monitoring network activity, and ensuring employees are aware of cybersecurity policies and risks.

By recognizing these **common threats**—from phishing to malware, ransomware, data breaches, and insider threats—individuals and businesses can begin to build a stronger foundation for their cybersecurity efforts. These threats exploit different weaknesses, but they all share a common objective: to gain unauthorized access to valuable information. Building awareness around these threats is the first step in creating an environment where people can proactively protect themselves and respond effectively to potential risks.

Through a mix of caution, good habits, and proactive security practices, individuals and organizations can create a robust line of defense that reduces their vulnerability in an increasingly digital world.

Chapter 2: Building Cybersecurity Foundations at Home

Essential Cyber Hygiene Practices are the foundational steps every individual and household can take to protect against a variety of cyber threats. Just as we maintain good hygiene for our physical health, cyber hygiene helps ensure the safety of our digital lives. These practices reduce vulnerabilities, making it more difficult for attackers to access personal information or compromise devices. Good cyber hygiene is a combination of consistent habits, vigilant monitoring, and practical safeguards. By developing these practices, households can create a first line of defense that keeps their digital spaces secure.

Password Management and Multi-Factor Authentication are essential components of cyber hygiene. Passwords serve as the primary barrier between personal data and unauthorized users, which makes having strong, unique passwords a critical defense.

A good password management strategy involves creating complex, varied passwords that are hard to guess but easy to manage. Avoid common mistakes like using "12345" or easily guessed words. Instead, opt for a mix of uppercase and lowercase letters, numbers, and symbols, aiming for at least twelve characters whenever possible. Passwords should be unique for each account, as reusing the same password across multiple sites creates a domino effect if one account is compromised.

To simplify managing multiple complex passwords, a password manager can be highly effective. Password managers securely store and generate strong passwords, eliminating the need to remember each one individually. They provide an encrypted vault for all login credentials, allowing users to easily access them with a master password. This approach reduces the temptation to reuse passwords or resort to simpler passwords for convenience. With a password manager, users only need to remember a single, strong master password, while the tool handles the rest.

Multi-Factor Authentication (MFA) adds an additional layer of security beyond passwords by requiring a second form of verification. This typically involves a one-time code sent to a mobile device or email, a fingerprint scan, or a face recognition check. Even if a password is compromised, MFA ensures that unauthorized users still cannot access the account without the second form of authentication. Many platforms offer MFA as an option, and enabling it for all accounts that support it is a best practice. This simple step greatly reduces the risk of unauthorized access and adds a vital layer of protection for personal information.

Device Security is equally important in maintaining a secure home environment.

Personal devices, such as smartphones, laptops, and tablets, contain a wealth of personal and sensitive data.

If compromised, they can become entry points for attackers. To protect these devices, users should always keep their operating systems, applications, and antivirus software up to date. Software updates often include security patches that address vulnerabilities that could otherwise be exploited by hackers. Enabling automatic updates is a good way to ensure that devices remain protected without requiring constant manual checks.

Another key element of device security is enabling strong access controls. Using complex passcodes, fingerprint recognition, or face unlock features adds an extra layer of security, particularly for mobile devices that are more easily lost or stolen. Additionally, it's wise to disable Bluetooth and Wi-Fi when they're not in use, as open connections can serve as potential entry points for attackers. Many devices also offer encryption options, which further protect the data on the device by making it unreadable to unauthorized users. These measures, though simple, can go a long way in keeping personal devices secure.

Network Security Basics are fundamental in establishing a protected digital environment at home. Since most devices are connected through a home network, ensuring that this network is secure is essential. A compromised network can lead to unauthorized access to any connected device, including personal computers, smart home systems, and mobile phones. By configuring network security correctly, households can significantly reduce their vulnerability to outside threats.

Router Configuration and Firewall Use are key elements of network security. The router is the gateway that connects your home to the internet, so it's important to change the default settings it comes with.

Most routers have a default username and password that are easy to find online, making them vulnerable if left unchanged. A good first step is to change the default credentials to a unique, strong password that only household members know. Additionally, ensure that your router's firmware is regularly updated to benefit from security patches provided by the manufacturer.

Firewalls are another critical layer of network protection. Firewalls monitor and control incoming and outgoing network traffic, acting as a barrier that filters out potentially harmful data from the internet. Many routers have built-in firewalls, and enabling these features can block unauthorized access attempts. Some users may also choose to install firewall software on individual devices for added security.

This double-layered approach helps keep both the network and the devices connected to it safe from various online threats.

Encryption and Data Protection play a vital role in safeguarding sensitive information, both on devices and during online transactions.

Encryption is the process of converting data into a code to prevent unauthorized access. When data is encrypted, it becomes unreadable to anyone without the decryption key, which significantly enhances security. Most modern devices, including smartphones and computers, come with built-in encryption options that can be enabled in the settings. Enabling this feature means that if a device is lost or stolen, the data on it will remain protected.

Data protection also extends to the way we handle sensitive information online. Avoid sharing personal or financial details over unsecured websites, which are identified by a lack of "https" in the URL. Secured websites use encryption to protect data as it's transmitted, making it safer for online transactions and interactions.

Additionally, consider using a virtual private network (VPN) when connecting to public Wi-Fi. VPNs encrypt internet traffic, protecting it from prying eyes and reducing the risk of data interception by malicious actors.

One often overlooked aspect of data protection is regular data backup. Backing up data to a secure location—whether it be an external hard drive or a cloud service—ensures that information can be restored in case of device failure, loss, or a ransomware attack. A good backup strategy includes keeping copies of important files in multiple locations and updating these backups regularly. This habit not only protects against accidental data loss but also provides peace of mind in the event of a cyberattack.

In summary, building cybersecurity foundations at home involves developing a set of consistent habits and implementing key security measures across devices, networks, and personal data.

Password management, multi-factor authentication, and device security are the bedrocks of a secure digital life. At the same time, securing your home network through proper router configuration, firewall use, and encryption adds robust protection for the entire household. By adhering to these cybersecurity foundations, individuals and families can enjoy the benefits of a connected world while minimizing the risks that come with it.

Chapter 3: Strengthening Social Media Security

Social Media Account Protection is crucial as social media platforms increasingly become central to our personal and professional lives. These accounts hold vast amounts of personal information, from birth dates to location histories, and even our closest connections. When social media accounts are compromised, cybercriminals can gain insights into our daily lives and use this information for various malicious purposes, including identity theft and social engineering. Strengthening the security of social media profiles not only protects individuals but also minimizes the risk to their families and friends.

One of the simplest yet most effective ways to secure social media accounts is by focusing on **Privacy Settings and Strong Passwords**.

Most social media platforms offer privacy controls that allow users to determine who can see their posts, friend lists, and personal information.

By limiting visibility to trusted contacts, users can minimize exposure to strangers who might attempt to exploit the shared information. For example, setting profiles to "private" on platforms like Instagram and limiting post visibility to "friends only" on Facebook can significantly reduce the chances of unwanted individuals accessing personal details.

Equally important is the use of strong, unique passwords for each social media account. A strong password should include a combination of upper and lower-case letters, numbers, and symbols, making it hard to guess or crack. Avoid using easily guessed information such as birth dates, pet names, or simple sequences like "12345." Ideally, each social media platform should have its own unique password, as reusing the same password across multiple accounts creates a single point of failure. If one account is compromised, attackers could potentially gain access to all other accounts that use the same password. Password managers can help users store complex, unique passwords securely, making it easier to maintain this practice.

Multi-factor authentication (MFA) is another essential feature to enable, as it requires a second form of verification, like a code sent to a mobile device, in addition to the password. This additional step ensures that even if a password is compromised, unauthorized users will have difficulty accessing the account without the second form of authentication. By setting up strong privacy controls and adopting robust password practices, users can build a solid defense around their social media profiles.

Recognizing Social Media Scams is another critical component of maintaining security.

Social media scams are constantly evolving, targeting users through fake messages, ads, and even friend requests. One common scam involves messages that appear to be from someone on the user's friends list, often claiming there's an emergency and requesting financial help. Another frequent scam involves "too good to be true" offers, where fake giveaways or contests are used to lure users into sharing personal information or clicking malicious links.

Other scams include phishing attempts where users receive a message prompting them to log in to their accounts via a provided link. These links often lead to fake login pages designed to steal credentials. Users should be cautious of any unsolicited message asking them to log in, especially if it claims that account access will be lost otherwise. Being vigilant about such messages, avoiding suspicious links, and reporting scams to the platform are effective ways to protect against social media scams.

Managing Connected Apps and Sharing Practices further strengthens social media security by addressing the risks associated with third-party integrations and shared information.

Many social media users unknowingly grant permissions to third-party apps when they take personality quizzes, participate in games, or use external services that integrate with their social profiles. These **Third-Party App Permissions** can expose account information to third parties, increasing vulnerability. Each third-party app connected to an account potentially has access to personal data, friend lists, and sometimes even the ability to post on the user's behalf.

Regularly reviewing and managing these third-party app permissions is crucial. Most social media platforms allow users to view a list of connected apps and remove access for any app that is no longer needed or looks suspicious.

By limiting the number of third-party apps with access to social media profiles, users reduce the risk of unauthorized data exposure. It's wise to avoid connecting unnecessary apps to social media accounts altogether and, if an app is truly necessary, to carefully read the permissions it requests before granting access.

Another significant aspect of social media security involves adopting **Safe Sharing Practices**. Social media encourages sharing, but oversharing can inadvertently provide useful information to cybercriminals. For example, sharing details about daily routines, vacation plans, or location check-ins can make users more vulnerable to stalking, theft, and social engineering attacks. Hackers can piece together information from various posts to build a profile of a person's habits, whereabouts, and connections, which can be exploited for malicious purposes.

Limiting personal information in profiles is a simple but effective strategy.

Avoid displaying birth dates, home addresses, and phone numbers publicly. Additionally, reconsider the use of location-sharing features. While it may be tempting to share a location during travel, it can also signal that your home is unoccupied. Sharing travel updates or location check-ins after the trip is a safer approach, reducing the risk of being targeted based on real-time location data. Parents should also exercise caution when sharing information or images of their children, as these posts can inadvertently expose them to risks.

For businesses and professionals, safe sharing extends to managing the visibility of work-related information. Sharing details about clients, projects, or work locations can unintentionally reveal sensitive information. For example, posts that showcase a project may give competitors or malicious actors insight into proprietary business processes or confidential client information.

To maintain both personal and professional safety, it's essential to think critically about each piece of information shared on social media, ensuring that it cannot be used in harmful ways.

In summary, strengthening social media security requires a combination of proactive measures and cautious behavior. By optimizing **social media account protection** through privacy settings, strong passwords, and multi-factor authentication, users can establish robust initial defenses. Recognizing the signs of social media scams helps individuals avoid common pitfalls that cybercriminals use to gain unauthorized access. Managing connected apps and adopting **safe sharing practices** adds another layer of protection by reducing exposure to risks associated with data access and oversharing.

Building a habit of regularly reviewing social media settings, permissions, and content can create a secure digital environment that protects personal information and reduces vulnerability. Social media is a powerful tool for connection and communication, but its security ultimately depends on the choices made by its users. By following these steps, individuals can enjoy the benefits of social media while minimizing the associated risks.

Chapter 4: Safeguarding Children Online

Educating Children on Digital Safety is essential in a world where the internet has become a primary space for learning, socializing, and entertainment. As children spend more time online, they face various risks, from inappropriate content and cyberbullying to stranger danger and data privacy issues. Building awareness of these risks from an early age empowers children to navigate the digital world safely. Teaching children about online threats requires a delicate balance between protection and freedom, helping them understand potential dangers without creating unnecessary fear.

Age-Appropriate Cyber Threat Awareness is a vital part of this education.

Children need guidance on recognizing online risks, but the way these lessons are delivered should be tailored to their age and comprehension level. For younger children, basic rules like "never talk to strangers online" or "ask before clicking on links" are foundational. At this age, it's also helpful to explain that not everything they see online is true or safe. Simple explanations about privacy, like not sharing personal information with anyone they don't know, can build early habits of caution and discretion.

For older children and teenagers, discussions around online risks can be more detailed. They should learn about cyberbullying, phishing, and even the potential risks of oversharing on social media. Teaching them to recognize suspicious messages or friend requests is essential, as many scams and inappropriate interactions are designed to exploit their curiosity and trust.

Older children can also benefit from understanding that their digital footprint is permanent, influencing how they choose to interact online. By building awareness of these risks, children develop a sense of digital responsibility that will serve them well into adulthood.

Parental Controls and Monitoring Tools provide additional layers of security, allowing parents to guide and protect their children's online experiences. Setting up controls on devices and apps gives parents the ability to filter content, restrict access to certain websites, and monitor screen time. While these tools are valuable, they work best when combined with open communication about their purpose. Children are often more receptive to rules when they understand that the intent is to keep them safe, not to invade their privacy.

Setting Up Parental Controls on devices and apps is straightforward on most major platforms. Many operating systems, such as iOS and Android, offer built-in parental controls that allow parents to set limits on screen time, block certain apps, and control in-app purchases. These settings can prevent children from accidentally accessing inappropriate content or spending money on games and apps. Social media platforms also have privacy settings that allow parents to restrict who can interact with their child's account, though parents should carefully assess which platforms are age-appropriate.

For gaming consoles, parental controls can limit online interactions, restricting voice chat or messaging features to prevent unwanted communication from strangers. Similarly, streaming services often include parental control features that allow parents to create separate profiles with specific content restrictions, ensuring that children can only view age-appropriate shows and movies.

Taking the time to configure these settings can significantly reduce the likelihood of children encountering harmful content or risky interactions online.

In addition to controls on individual devices, parents may also want to consider network-level protection. Many home routers offer parental control features that allow parents to set restrictions on all devices connected to the network. By managing settings directly through the router, parents can block specific websites, schedule internet access times, and even monitor traffic to see which sites and apps are most frequently used. These controls provide a higher level of supervision without the need to modify settings on every individual device, making it a convenient solution for households with multiple users.

Encouraging Responsible Online Behavior is the final piece of the puzzle in ensuring children's online safety.

While parental controls and monitoring tools provide important safeguards, teaching children to adopt good digital habits is invaluable for long-term protection. Helping children understand the importance of online etiquette, privacy, and critical thinking gives them a foundation for responsible internet use that they will carry into adulthood.

One way to promote responsible behavior is by setting clear guidelines on acceptable online interactions. Encouraging children to treat others with respect online—just as they would in person—can help reduce the likelihood of them engaging in or becoming targets of cyberbullying. It's also essential to talk about the consequences of their actions online. Children need to understand that what they post, share, or comment on can have a lasting impact on their reputation.

Teaching them to pause and think before sharing content, especially personal information, can reduce impulsive decisions that might lead to regret.

Open discussions about privacy and sharing are also crucial. Children should be encouraged to keep certain information private, such as their full name, school, address, and phone number. They should understand that strangers or even acquaintances online do not need to know every detail about their lives. Creating a family rule, such as not sharing photos or personal updates without permission, can instill a habit of caution. If children know that certain boundaries apply, they're more likely to think twice before oversharing.

Helping children recognize and report suspicious or uncomfortable online interactions is another important aspect of responsible behavior. By teaching them to identify inappropriate messages or friend requests, parents empower children to protect themselves.

Encourage children to come to a trusted adult if they experience anything online that feels wrong or makes them uncomfortable. Building a culture of openness and trust ensures that children feel safe seeking help rather than hiding incidents out of fear or embarrassment.

Lastly, setting a positive example is one of the most effective ways to encourage responsible online behavior. Children often model their behavior after adults, so demonstrating good cybersecurity habits, such as being cautious with online information, using strong passwords, and limiting screen time, can reinforce these practices. If children see that their parents value online safety, they're more likely to adopt similar behaviors and understand the importance of these precautions.

In summary, **safeguarding children online** is a combination of education, tools, and guidance.

By building **age-appropriate cyber threat awareness**, parents help their children recognize potential risks and develop the critical thinking skills needed to navigate the internet safely.

Parental controls and monitoring tools add valuable layers of protection, reducing exposure to harmful content and interactions. **Encouraging responsible online behavior** empowers children to make safe, respectful choices as they explore the digital world. With these measures in place, parents can create an online environment that balances safety with the freedom for children to learn, socialize, and grow.

Chapter 5: Protecting Vulnerable Family Members

Digital Safety for Vulnerable Adults is an essential part of ensuring that all family members can use technology securely and responsibly. As more of our lives move online, vulnerable adults—such as elderly family members, individuals with limited digital experience, or those with cognitive impairments—may find themselves at higher risk for online exploitation. Cybercriminals often target these individuals because they may be less familiar with the tactics commonly used to gain access to sensitive information or persuade them into financial transactions.

Protecting vulnerable adults requires a combination of awareness, tools, and ongoing support, helping them safely navigate the online environment.

Identifying and Mitigating Risks is the first step in protecting vulnerable family members.

One of the most common forms of online exploitation is fraud, which can take many forms, from phishing emails that attempt to steal passwords to fake charity requests designed to collect donations under false pretenses. Vulnerable adults may also encounter scams that impersonate legitimate companies, such as tech support services, where attackers pretend to be representatives from well-known technology companies and claim that there's a problem with the victim's computer. This tactic can be particularly effective, as the scammers often use fear and urgency to prompt immediate action.

To recognize signs of online exploitation, it's important to look out for unusual financial activity, such as sudden transfers, unexplained credit card charges, or frequent purchases.

Unfamiliar devices or apps on their computers, unexpected pop-ups, or messages prompting them to call unfamiliar numbers can also signal potential scams.

If vulnerable family members frequently share information about unsolicited phone calls, emails, or social media messages, it's essential to investigate further. Educating them about common warning signs, like messages that ask for immediate payments, requests for sensitive information, or offers that seem too good to be true, can help them spot scams before they fall victim to them.

Setting up safeguards to limit access to financial accounts and personal information can further reduce risk. For example, family members can encourage vulnerable adults to limit online banking access to a single, well-secured device, use strong passwords, and enable two-factor authentication (2FA) on important accounts.

Regularly checking for unauthorized charges or account changes, with permission, can provide an additional layer of oversight and catch suspicious activity early.

Digital Estate and Account Management is another critical consideration in protecting vulnerable adults. In today's digital age, nearly everyone has an assortment of online accounts and digital assets, from social media profiles to email accounts, cloud storage, and even online banking. Managing these digital assets becomes increasingly challenging if someone is unable to remember account details or handle their own digital affairs due to cognitive or physical limitations. Planning for these scenarios can save families from significant stress and ensure that essential digital assets are managed responsibly.

Planning for Digital Assets involves creating a record of online accounts and their respective access information, such as usernames, passwords, and security questions.

This record should be stored in a secure location, like a password manager or a physical, locked document. Some families choose to use digital estate planning tools or appoint a trusted person to serve as a "digital executor," who will manage these accounts if the vulnerable adult is unable to do so. Ideally, this person should have a clear understanding of the digital landscape and a close relationship with the individual they're helping.

In some cases, setting up emergency access for essential accounts, such as email or social media, may be beneficial. Many email providers and social media platforms offer options to designate a trusted contact who can access an account if needed. By enabling these settings, vulnerable adults can be assured that their accounts will be handled responsibly should the need arise. It's also wise to review and consolidate online accounts, closing unused profiles or services that could present unnecessary security risks.

Protecting from Scams is a key aspect of digital safety for vulnerable adults.

Many adults who are new to digital devices or online services may be unaware of common scams and feel pressured or confused by unexpected requests. Training them to recognize and avoid scams can empower them to navigate online spaces more confidently. Start by explaining the importance of not sharing personal or financial information with anyone they don't know and emphasizing that legitimate companies will never ask for sensitive data through unsolicited messages or phone calls.

Encourage them to be skeptical of any message, email, or phone call that creates a sense of urgency or fear. Scammers often use language that pressures the recipient into acting immediately, warning of consequences if they don't respond quickly. This tactic is particularly common in tech support scams, where scammers claim that a computer has been compromised and needs immediate repair. Vulnerable adults should know that they can always contact a trusted family member or friend if they are unsure about a message or request.

Additionally, it's helpful to set up security measures that reduce the chances of falling victim to scams. For example, enabling spam filters on their email accounts can prevent many phishing emails from reaching their inbox. Installing reputable antivirus software on their devices provides a layer of protection against malware and other malicious programs that might be inadvertently downloaded. Pop-up blockers can also be beneficial, as many scams rely on pop-ups that mimic security warnings or display false error messages.

Discussing the risks of online shopping is also important. Many scams target individuals through fake online stores or counterfeit products, luring them into providing credit card details or other personal information.

Teaching vulnerable adults to shop only from reputable websites and to look for secure connections (indicated by a lock icon or "https" in the web address) can minimize these risks. Encouraging them to use secure payment methods, such as credit cards or trusted payment platforms, rather than debit cards or direct bank transfers, offers additional protection.

In some situations, setting up a family member as a "trusted contact" for bank accounts or important online accounts can serve as an additional safety net. This person can assist with monitoring account activity, reporting suspicious transactions, and providing guidance when questionable situations arise. Such measures can give both the vulnerable adult and their family peace of mind, knowing that support is readily available if needed.

In summary, protecting vulnerable family members online involves multiple layers of support, from recognizing **signs of online**

exploitation to effectively managing **digital assets and accounts**. By providing the tools and knowledge needed to navigate the digital world, families can help vulnerable adults avoid scams, preserve their privacy, and maintain control over their online activities. The goal is not only to protect but also to empower, ensuring that these family members can experience the benefits of technology safely and confidently.

Chapter 6: Preparing for a Cyberattack

Recognizing Signs of a Cyberattack is a vital skill in today's increasingly digital world. Detecting the early signs of an attack can mean the difference between a quick response that minimizes damage and a delayed reaction that allows an attacker to cause extensive harm. Cyberattacks don't always announce themselves in obvious ways; they often begin subtly, with slight changes or unusual behavior on devices that may go unnoticed. Understanding these warning signs can help individuals and organizations take immediate steps to protect their data and devices.

Common Warning Indicators of a cyberattack include a range of unusual activities that can point to unauthorized access or malicious software.

One of the most evident signs is a sudden slowdown in device performance. While computers, phones, or tablets may slow down for various reasons, a drastic and unexplained decrease in speed could suggest malware running in the background. Malware, such as spyware or ransomware, often consumes resources as it collects data or encrypts files, causing the device to lag significantly.

Unexpected pop-ups or error messages are also key warning signs. Many forms of malware generate fake system warnings or error messages, often asking the user to click on a link or download a "fix." These pop-ups may look like legitimate system alerts, but they're designed to lure users into downloading more malicious software or revealing personal information. Another red flag is the appearance of unfamiliar programs or applications.

If new software appears without the user's knowledge or consent, it's essential to investigate further, as it could be a form of malware installed by an attacker.

Suspicious network activity is another indicator of a potential attack. Unusual outgoing traffic, especially to unknown IP addresses, may indicate that a device has been compromised and is sending data to an external server. Monitoring network activity and checking for unknown connections can help identify such issues early. Additionally, unexpected login attempts or password change notifications for accounts are often signs of unauthorized access. Cybercriminals may try to change passwords to lock out the original user, so any unfamiliar notifications should be treated seriously.

Strange behavior in email or messaging accounts is also a warning sign. If contacts report receiving unusual messages from an account, it could mean that a cybercriminal has gained access and is using the account to send spam or phishing messages.

Users should be wary of unexpected emails that request sensitive information, contain suspicious attachments, or link to unfamiliar websites. Recognizing these signs early and reacting quickly is the first step in minimizing the impact of a cyberattack.

Emergency Action Plan is essential for responding to a cyberattack effectively and minimizing the damage. Having a plan in place allows individuals and organizations to act swiftly, reducing the time attackers have to exploit vulnerabilities. Preparing for an attack involves setting up clear, predefined steps that anyone can follow, ensuring a coordinated response even under pressure. A well-structured emergency action plan doesn't need to be complex, but it should be comprehensive and accessible.

Steps to Take if Attacked should begin with disconnecting affected devices from the internet or any network.

This action is crucial because it isolates the device, preventing further data transmission to the attacker or the spread of malware to other devices. Whether the suspected attack is on a personal device or a business network, immediate disconnection is a primary step in halting the attack. In a business setting, employees should know how to disconnect devices quickly and alert the IT department to contain the threat.

Next, it's important to notify the appropriate individuals or teams. In personal cases, this may mean contacting any service providers related to the compromised account, such as a bank for financial breaches or an email provider for account access issues. For businesses, notifying the IT or cybersecurity team as soon as possible ensures that professionals can assess the situation and deploy countermeasures.

Prompt communication is essential, as cybersecurity teams need detailed information to respond effectively. Some organizations also have security incident response teams trained specifically to handle cyber threats, making them valuable first responders during an attack.

After securing the device and notifying key contacts, consider running an antivirus or malware scan if it's safe to do so. This scan can help identify and remove malicious software. However, in some cases, attempting to clean an infected device immediately may interfere with ongoing investigations or damage evidence, so it's best to consult with cybersecurity experts before taking further action. Businesses, in particular, should consult IT professionals who can determine the best course of action without compromising evidence that may later aid in identifying the attacker.

Documenting the Incident is an often-overlooked but crucial step in responding to a cyberattack. Creating a detailed record of the incident can provide valuable information for future prevention and help with any legal or forensic investigations that may follow. Documenting the attack begins with noting the initial signs or symptoms observed. This might include the first unusual message received, a screenshot of a suspicious pop-up, or a record of any unfamiliar programs that appeared.

The documentation process should include timestamps, noting the exact times when suspicious activity was first noticed, when devices were disconnected, and when notifications were sent to relevant individuals. This timeline can help cybersecurity experts trace the sequence of events and better understand how the attack progressed. Keeping records of all communications related to the attack is also important. For example, saving emails or messages from attackers, even if they are suspected phishing attempts, can provide clues about their methods and motives.

Additionally, document any actions taken in response to the attack.

This includes steps such as disconnecting devices, contacting IT teams, and running scans. Detailed records ensure that nothing is overlooked and can provide insights into what worked well and what might need improvement for future incidents. Many organizations have standardized incident report forms that guide employees in capturing all relevant information. For individuals, creating a simple written or digital report covering the main points is sufficient.

In some cases, it may be necessary to report the attack to external authorities. Certain types of cybercrimes, such as fraud, identity theft, or data breaches, require reporting to law enforcement or regulatory agencies. For example, businesses that handle customer data may be legally obligated to notify affected individuals and data protection authorities in the event of a breach.

Knowing the reporting requirements in advance and incorporating them into the action plan can streamline the process and ensure compliance.

In summary, **preparing for a cyberattack** is about recognizing early warning signs, having a well-defined emergency action plan, and ensuring thorough documentation. Understanding **common warning indicators** like suspicious device behavior or strange messages helps in detecting attacks quickly. Implementing a solid **emergency action plan** with clear steps, including disconnecting devices and notifying relevant parties, minimizes potential damage.

Lastly, **documenting the incident** provides essential information for investigation and prevention, helping individuals and organizations build resilience against future cyber threats. Being prepared empowers people to act confidently and effectively when faced with a cyberattack, reducing the likelihood of severe consequences.

Chapter 7: Responding to Specific Cyberattacks

Phishing and Social Engineering Attacks are among the most common and effective types of cyberattacks because they exploit human psychology rather than technical vulnerabilities. Phishing attacks typically involve emails, messages, or websites that appear legitimate, tricking users into revealing sensitive information like passwords or credit card details. Social engineering goes beyond traditional phishing, employing tactics to manipulate individuals into performing actions that compromise security, such as transferring money or divulging confidential information.

The key to mitigating the effects of these attacks lies in recognizing and responding swiftly.

Immediate Response Steps are critical when a phishing or social engineering attack is detected.

If you realize you've clicked on a phishing link, do not provide any additional information or complete any actions requested by the attacker. Close the browser immediately, disconnect from the internet, and avoid further interactions with the suspicious content. Next, change the password associated with the account that may have been compromised, and make sure to create a strong, unique password that hasn't been used before. If multi-factor authentication (MFA) is available, enable it to add an extra layer of security.

In a business setting, notify the IT or security team as soon as a phishing or social engineering attack is identified. This allows cybersecurity professionals to conduct further assessments and determine whether any systems have been compromised.

Reporting the attack to the platform or service provider, such as email or social media, can also help prevent similar attacks on others. Finally, conduct a security scan on your device to check for any malware that may have been installed as part of the phishing attack. Regularly reviewing security settings and running scans helps ensure no residual effects from the incident.

Handling Ransomware Attacks requires careful consideration of recovery options and an understanding of the risks associated with different responses. Ransomware is a type of malware that encrypts files, rendering them inaccessible until a ransom is paid. Ransomware attacks can be devastating, especially for individuals or businesses with limited backup systems in place. Deciding how to respond to a ransomware attack involves evaluating available recovery options and the potential consequences of each choice.

Recovery Options and Risks of Paying the ransom should be carefully weighed.

In many cases, cybersecurity experts and law enforcement strongly advise against paying the ransom, as there is no guarantee that attackers will provide the decryption key or unlock the files. Paying the ransom also perpetuates the cycle, potentially encouraging attackers to target more victims. For organizations, paying a ransom can also lead to reputational damage, as it may signal to customers that they were unprepared for such an incident.

The first step in recovery is to isolate the affected device from the network, preventing the ransomware from spreading to other systems. Next, assess whether recent backups are available, as restoring data from a backup is often the safest and most reliable recovery method. If backups are accessible, ensure they are clean by running a thorough malware scan before restoring them to the system.

For businesses, having a disaster recovery plan in place can streamline the restoration process, minimizing downtime and data loss.

If backups are unavailable, consult with cybersecurity professionals who specialize in ransomware recovery. They may be able to assist with data recovery efforts or help identify possible workarounds. In some cases, decryption tools for specific ransomware strains may be available through trusted cybersecurity resources or law enforcement agencies. Organizations like No More Ransom offer free decryption tools for certain types of ransomware, potentially allowing victims to recover their data without paying the attackers.

Data Breach Responses are essential when sensitive information, such as personal, financial, or proprietary data, is exposed or stolen. Data breaches can occur due to weak passwords, phishing attacks, or system vulnerabilities.

When a data breach is detected, responding quickly is critical to prevent further exposure, contain the breach, and secure the compromised data.

Securing Compromised Data involves several steps, starting with isolating the affected systems to prevent unauthorized access from spreading. Change passwords immediately for any compromised accounts and enable multi-factor authentication (MFA) to strengthen security. Conduct a thorough audit to determine the extent of the breach and identify the specific data that has been exposed. If you detect unusual activity in any accounts or applications linked to the breach, take steps to secure them as well, such as updating login credentials and reviewing recent account activity for unauthorized actions.

In a business environment, notify the cybersecurity team or engage external cybersecurity experts to conduct a forensic analysis.

This investigation helps determine how the breach occurred and what data was affected, providing essential information for risk mitigation.

Organizations should also consider legal and regulatory requirements regarding data protection, as many regions mandate specific actions, such as notifying affected individuals and data protection authorities. Regularly updating security protocols and conducting staff training on cybersecurity best practices are also valuable steps to prevent future breaches.

Notifying Affected Parties is an important part of data breach response, as it provides transparency and enables those affected to take protective measures. If the breach involves customer data, notifying affected parties promptly is both a legal obligation and an ethical responsibility. Many jurisdictions, including the European Union under the General Data Protection Regulation (GDPR) and certain U.S. states, require organizations to inform affected individuals within a specific timeframe after a breach is confirmed.

When notifying affected individuals, communicate clearly about the nature of the breach, the type of information exposed, and steps they can take to protect themselves. For example, if financial information was compromised, advise affected individuals to monitor their accounts for suspicious activity, consider freezing their credit, and change passwords for related accounts. Providing resources such as customer support contact information and links to helpful websites on identity protection can help ease concerns and demonstrate a commitment to security.

Additionally, for organizations, notifying regulatory bodies may be necessary to comply with data protection laws. Regulatory authorities often have specific guidelines on what should be reported, which may include the nature of the breach, the estimated number of individuals affected, and the steps being taken to contain and mitigate the incident. Fulfilling these reporting requirements can help avoid penalties and build trust with customers by showing that the organization is taking the breach seriously and working to resolve it responsibly.

In summary, **responding to specific cyberattacks** like phishing, ransomware, and data breaches requires prompt action, clear protocols, and effective communication. In cases of **phishing and social engineering attacks**, immediate response steps, such as closing affected accounts and conducting device scans, can help contain the threat. For **handling ransomware attacks**, isolating the device, exploring recovery options, and consulting professionals are crucial, while careful consideration of the risks of paying the ransom is essential.

When it comes to **data breach responses**, securing compromised data and promptly

notifying affected parties are necessary to minimize harm and prevent further damage. By understanding these steps and implementing a clear, well-practiced response plan, individuals and organizations can protect themselves more effectively, reduce the potential impact of these attacks, and strengthen their resilience against future threats.

Chapter 8: Recovery and Rebuilding After an Attack

System Restoration and Data Recovery are crucial steps after a cyberattack, as they enable individuals and organizations to regain access to their systems and resume normal operations. Recovering from an attack requires a systematic approach to restore functionality while ensuring that no traces of malware or vulnerabilities remain. The process begins with carefully restoring data from secure backups and performing a thorough check to confirm that systems are clean and stable.

Using Backups for Recovery is often the safest and most efficient method for restoring systems after an attack. Regular backups allow users to retrieve data from a specific point before the attack occurred, minimizing data loss and disruption.

When restoring from backups, it's essential to use the most recent backup that was created prior to the incident, as any backups created after the attack may also contain compromised data or malware. Keeping multiple versions of backups can be beneficial in such cases, as it provides more flexibility in selecting a clean, unaffected backup.

It's also important to verify the integrity of backups before restoration. Running malware scans on backup files ensures that they are free of malicious software, preventing reinfection when restored to the system. For businesses, having an organized, reliable backup strategy in place, such as the 3-2-1 rule (three copies of data, stored on two different media, with one copy offsite), can streamline the recovery process and minimize data loss.

Following best practices in backup management—like scheduling automated backups, periodically testing restoration processes, and storing backups in secure locations—can significantly reduce the time required to recover after an attack.

Once the data is restored, it's essential to verify system functionality by testing core applications and services to ensure they are operating correctly. This includes checking critical applications, network connectivity, and user access permissions. By carefully following these steps, individuals and organizations can confidently restore their systems, knowing they have taken measures to prevent reinfection and data loss.

Running Post-Attack Security Scans is the next step to confirm that no remnants of the attack remain in the system. Attackers often leave behind traces of malware or backdoors, which are unauthorized access points that allow them to re-enter the system. Conducting a full security scan after data restoration helps identify and remove any lingering threats.

Antivirus and anti-malware software can detect and quarantine malicious files, while firewall logs and network monitoring tools can highlight any unusual activity that may signal unauthorized access attempts.

In addition to running antivirus and anti-malware scans, checking system configurations is essential to verify that no unauthorized changes were made. For example, attackers may alter security settings or create new user accounts to maintain access to the system. Reviewing these settings and user accounts helps ensure that attackers have no way of regaining access.

For businesses, cybersecurity professionals may recommend deeper forensic analysis, which examines system logs, network traffic, and user behavior to uncover hidden threats or understand how the attack occurred. These scans provide confidence that systems are fully secure and allow users to rebuild on a solid foundation.

Reviewing Security Weaknesses is a critical part of the recovery process, as it enables individuals and organizations to learn from the incident and strengthen their defenses for the future.

Conducting a post-mortem analysis provides insight into how the attack happened, what vulnerabilities were exploited, and what steps can be taken to prevent similar incidents. This evaluation is especially valuable for organizations, as it can highlight gaps in cybersecurity practices, such as outdated software, insufficient employee training, or inadequate security protocols.

Learning from the Incident involves gathering data from various sources, including system logs, employee reports, and forensic analyses, to create a comprehensive view of the attack. Reviewing this information allows individuals and teams to understand the sequence of events that led to the breach, identifying specific weaknesses that contributed to the attack's success. It's helpful to answer questions like: How did the attacker gain access? Were there missed warning signs? Could any steps have been taken sooner to prevent the attack from escalating?

For businesses, a post-mortem analysis often involves a collaborative review with input from IT staff, management, and any other stakeholders involved in the response. Documenting these findings in a formal report ensures that everyone understands the lessons learned and the specific actions needed to enhance security. Some organizations choose to conduct "lessons learned" meetings to discuss the attack in detail, allowing employees to contribute insights and gain a better understanding of cybersecurity risks. This collaborative approach fosters a culture of continuous improvement, encouraging proactive measures to prevent future incidents.

Updating Security Measures based on insights from the incident is the final step in rebuilding a more resilient system. This involves implementing concrete changes to address the vulnerabilities identified during the post-mortem analysis.

Updating security measures may include upgrading software, changing security configurations, or adopting new cybersecurity tools. For example, if the attack occurred due to a phishing email, implementing stronger email filtering and training employees on recognizing phishing attempts can reduce the likelihood of future incidents.

Regularly updating software and applying security patches is one of the most effective ways to prevent cyberattacks, as many attacks exploit known vulnerabilities in outdated software. Ensuring that all devices and applications are set to update automatically helps maintain a secure environment. For businesses, reviewing and updating security policies, such as access control protocols and password management guidelines, can address specific weaknesses that may have been exploited in the attack. Enhancing multi-factor authentication (MFA) practices and limiting administrative access can further reduce risk.

Strengthening employee awareness and training is another key aspect of updating security measures. For organizations, employees are often the first line of defense, and their ability to recognize and respond to potential threats is critical. Providing regular training on cybersecurity best practices, including identifying phishing attempts and using secure communication methods, empowers employees to make informed decisions and take proactive steps to protect company data.

Finally, consider adopting advanced security solutions, such as intrusion detection systems, endpoint protection platforms, and vulnerability scanning tools. These tools can help detect and respond to threats more effectively, ensuring that any unusual activity is quickly identified and addressed. For businesses, partnering with a managed security service provider (MSSP) can offer ongoing support, monitoring, and expertise to maintain a secure environment.

In summary, **recovery and rebuilding after an attack** involve a series of structured steps designed to restore system integrity, eliminate remaining threats, and strengthen defenses for the future. **System restoration and data recovery** through secure backups and post-attack scans ensures that systems are operational and clean. By **reviewing security weaknesses** through a detailed post-mortem analysis, individuals and organizations can gain valuable insights into how the attack occurred and identify areas for improvement.

Finally, **updating security measures** based on lessons learned creates a more resilient system, reducing the likelihood of future attacks and empowering users to navigate the digital world with confidence.

Through these recovery steps, individuals and organizations can not only recover from an attack but also emerge stronger and better prepared for the evolving cyber threat landscape.

Chapter 9: Developing a Long-Term Cybersecurity Plan

Creating and Maintaining Security Policies is the foundation of a strong cybersecurity plan. Policies provide a structured approach to protecting data, devices, and networks, setting clear guidelines for handling digital assets and managing potential risks. A well-designed security policy framework supports a proactive approach to cybersecurity, establishing best practices that individuals and organizations can follow to minimize vulnerabilities.

For both home users and small businesses, developing and maintaining these policies is essential for long-term protection and resilience.

Policy Framework for Home and Small Business involves creating specific guidelines that address the unique needs and risks faced by households and smaller organizations.

At home, a security policy framework might include basic guidelines like using strong, unique passwords for all accounts, setting up multi-factor authentication (MFA), and avoiding suspicious links and downloads. For families, the framework could also incorporate rules about device use, such as restricting access to certain websites or limiting screen time for younger members. These simple rules can help maintain a secure digital environment by establishing safe practices for everyone in the household.

For small businesses, a policy framework is typically more comprehensive, covering areas such as data storage, access controls, and software usage. This framework should outline how employees are expected to handle sensitive data, who has access to critical systems, and how to respond to potential security threats.

Policies for small businesses might include rules on employee device management, such as requiring encryption on laptops and mobile devices used for work, and ensuring that all work-related data is stored on secure, approved platforms. Additionally, it's wise to include clear guidelines on social media usage, remote work protocols, and network security, as these areas often present higher risks.

Maintaining these policies requires regular review and updates, especially as technology and threats evolve. Designating a specific person to oversee cybersecurity policy management ensures that policies are consistently enforced and that any necessary adjustments are promptly implemented. This proactive approach minimizes risks by adapting to emerging cybersecurity challenges.

Regular Security Audits are essential for keeping cybersecurity defenses effective over time.

A security audit is a systematic review of an organization's practices, policies, and systems to identify vulnerabilities and ensure compliance with established security standards. Regular audits help uncover gaps or weaknesses that may have gone unnoticed, providing an opportunity to strengthen security measures before they can be exploited by attackers.

For both home users and small businesses, software updates play a significant role in maintaining security. Software developers regularly release patches to fix known vulnerabilities, making updates a crucial part of an effective cybersecurity plan. Scheduling automatic updates for operating systems, applications, and antivirus software reduces the chances of running outdated, vulnerable versions.

Regularly reviewing access controls and network configurations also contributes to a secure environment, as it ensures that only authorized users have access to sensitive data and systems.

For businesses, periodic audits conducted by a third-party cybersecurity firm can provide additional insights and verify that all security measures are functioning as intended. These external audits offer an unbiased evaluation of the organization's cybersecurity health and help identify potential improvements. Regular audits reinforce a culture of continuous improvement, ensuring that security measures keep pace with evolving threats and industry standards.

Incident Response Planning is another critical element of a long-term cybersecurity strategy. Having a clear, actionable plan for responding to cybersecurity incidents allows individuals and businesses to react quickly, reducing the impact of an attack.

An incident response plan (IRP) outlines the steps to take when a threat is detected, including how to contain, investigate, and mitigate the damage caused by an attack. A well-developed IRP provides peace of mind, knowing that if an attack occurs, there's a predefined process in place to address it.

Establishing a Response Team (if applicable) can greatly enhance the effectiveness of an incident response plan, particularly for small businesses. A response team is a designated group of individuals trained to handle cybersecurity incidents. The team typically includes IT staff, security experts, and key decision-makers who can coordinate a swift, organized response.

In smaller businesses without dedicated cybersecurity staff, it may be beneficial to appoint a few individuals who receive basic cybersecurity training and can act as first responders in case of an incident.

The primary responsibilities of the response team include assessing the severity of the attack, implementing containment measures, and initiating recovery processes.

Team members should be familiar with common cyber threats, understand how to secure compromised systems, and know how to communicate effectively with other staff members. Regular training and simulations help the response team stay prepared, enabling them to respond confidently and efficiently to real incidents. In situations where an in-house response team isn't feasible, small businesses may consider partnering with an external cybersecurity service provider to support their incident response needs.

Disaster Recovery Plan is a critical component of cybersecurity planning, focusing on business continuity in the event of a major attack. Unlike the incident response plan, which addresses immediate containment and mitigation, the disaster recovery plan (DRP) is designed to restore operations and minimize downtime after an attack. The DRP details the steps for recovering data, restoring systems, and resuming normal business functions, ensuring that the organization can continue to operate even if core systems are affected.

For small businesses, a DRP often includes backup and restoration procedures, identifying key systems that must be prioritized for recovery, and establishing communication protocols for keeping employees and clients informed. Regularly testing the disaster recovery plan through simulated scenarios is essential for verifying its effectiveness. These tests ensure that all team members understand their roles, that the plan is feasible, and that any areas requiring improvement are addressed before a real disaster occurs.

In a home setting, a disaster recovery plan might include maintaining up-to-date backups of important files, knowing how to restore devices from backup, and having contact information for service providers or technical support if outside help is needed. While the scale of a DRP for individuals is generally smaller than that for a business, the objective remains the same: to ensure data integrity, maintain access to essential services, and recover quickly from disruptions.

In summary, **developing a long-term cybersecurity plan** involves establishing and maintaining strong security policies, conducting regular audits, and preparing for potential incidents through structured response and recovery plans. A solid **policy framework for home and small business** creates the foundation for consistent cybersecurity practices, addressing how data and devices should be managed and protected. **Regular security audits** help identify and address vulnerabilities, keeping defenses up-to-date and effective.

By developing a clear **incident response plan** and, if possible, **establishing a**

response team, individuals and businesses are better equipped to handle cybersecurity threats. Finally, a robust **disaster recovery plan** ensures that operations can continue and data can be restored after an attack. Together, these components form a comprehensive approach to long-term cybersecurity, fostering resilience and adaptability in an ever-changing digital landscape.

Chapter 10: Staying Updated on Cybersecurity Trends and Threats

Monitoring Emerging Cyber Threats is an essential practice in maintaining a strong cybersecurity posture, as the landscape of digital threats is constantly evolving. New vulnerabilities, hacking techniques, and malicious software emerge regularly, posing risks that require ongoing awareness and adaptation. Staying informed about these changes can help individuals and organizations anticipate potential threats and adjust their defenses accordingly. By making it a priority to track cybersecurity trends, users can stay one step ahead, ensuring that they are prepared to address new challenges as they arise.

Staying Informed requires a proactive approach, incorporating various tools and resources to keep up-to-date with the latest developments in cybersecurity.

One effective way to stay informed is by subscribing to cybersecurity newsletters from reputable sources, such as government cybersecurity agencies, cybersecurity firms, and industry organizations. These newsletters often provide insights into recent incidents, alerts about emerging threats, and expert analysis on trending issues. Additionally, signing up for email alerts from trusted sources like the Cybersecurity and Infrastructure Security Agency (CISA) or the Federal Trade Commission (FTC) ensures that important updates reach users promptly.

Following cybersecurity blogs and news sites is another useful strategy. Websites like Krebs on Security, Threatpost, and Dark Reading provide timely information on recent attacks, vulnerabilities, and other security news.

Regularly reading these sources helps individuals and businesses understand the real-world impact of cybersecurity incidents, offering lessons that can be applied to their own security practices. Many of these platforms offer analysis on how attacks were carried out, the vulnerabilities exploited, and the steps organizations took to mitigate damage, providing valuable insights for all readers.

Social media can also serve as a valuable source for tracking cybersecurity trends. Platforms like Twitter and LinkedIn host cybersecurity experts and professionals who frequently share insights, articles, and advice. Following these experts allows users to see updates as they happen and gain access to a wide range of perspectives on current security topics.

Cybersecurity communities on social media, such as cybersecurity subreddits or LinkedIn groups, foster discussions that provide a real-time exchange of information and strategies. Engaging with these communities can deepen one's understanding of cybersecurity trends and encourage active learning.

Continuing Education and Resources are crucial for anyone committed to maintaining effective cybersecurity practices over time. As the threat landscape changes, it's essential to keep building knowledge and skills that enable effective responses to new risks. Formal training programs, certifications, and online courses offer structured ways to enhance cybersecurity expertise, allowing users to learn at their own pace and according to their specific needs.

Training Opportunities are available for all levels, from beginners to advanced cybersecurity professionals. For those new to cybersecurity, introductory courses on platforms like Coursera, Udemy, and LinkedIn Learning cover foundational topics such as network security, data protection, and threat awareness. These courses provide a solid grounding in the essentials and are accessible to individuals and small business owners alike. For more in-depth knowledge, certifications offer recognized credentials that signal a strong understanding of cybersecurity practices.

The CompTIA Security+ certification is an excellent entry-level credential for those interested in building core security skills, covering topics such as threat management, cryptography, and risk management. For those seeking more advanced knowledge, certifications like Certified Information Systems Security Professional (CISSP) and Certified Ethical Hacker (CEH) dive deeper into specialized areas, such as ethical hacking, penetration testing, and security auditing.

These certifications are widely recognized in the industry and help professionals build practical skills that are immediately applicable to real-world scenarios.

Ongoing training is particularly valuable for businesses, as employees play a critical role in maintaining cybersecurity.

Many companies choose to implement regular cybersecurity training sessions for their staff, ensuring that everyone is aware of current threats and knows how to respond appropriately. In addition to formal training, some organizations conduct phishing simulations or cybersecurity drills to reinforce awareness and keep employees engaged. For small businesses, encouraging employees to pursue basic cybersecurity courses and certifications can enhance the overall security of the organization.

Community Engagement and Support is another powerful resource for staying current with cybersecurity trends. Engaging with online communities, forums, and government resources allows individuals and businesses to share experiences, ask questions, and access expert advice. Cybersecurity forums, such as the ones on Reddit (like r/cybersecurity) or specialized websites like Stack Overflow, provide spaces where users can discuss security-related topics, troubleshoot issues, and receive feedback from knowledgeable peers. These forums are also excellent places to learn about common cybersecurity challenges and the solutions that others have implemented.

Government resources offer reliable, accessible information that can help users stay informed about cybersecurity best practices. Many governments have dedicated cybersecurity agencies that publish guidelines, alerts, and reports to help the public understand and respond to cyber threats. In the United States, CISA offers a range of resources, including free training materials, threat advisories, and toolkits for individuals and businesses.

For example, CISA's cybersecurity alerts provide real-time notifications of emerging threats, helping users take timely precautions.

The National Institute of Standards and Technology (NIST) also provides comprehensive resources for small businesses, such as the Cybersecurity Framework, which outlines best practices for managing cybersecurity risks.

Participating in cybersecurity-focused events, such as webinars, conferences, and workshops, is another valuable way to stay informed and engaged. Many conferences, like Black Hat and DEFCON, host sessions that showcase the latest developments in cybersecurity and allow participants to hear directly from experts. Some of these events are held virtually, making them accessible to a global audience. Attending these events provides opportunities to learn about cutting-edge technology, emerging threats, and innovative solutions, all of which can contribute to a deeper understanding of the cybersecurity field.

Cybersecurity support groups and mentoring programs can also help individuals stay updated and build confidence. Mentorship programs, such as those offered by the International Association of Cybersecurity Professionals (IACP), connect newcomers with experienced professionals who provide guidance, answer questions, and offer career advice. This support can be invaluable for individuals looking to advance their skills and knowledge while building a professional network in the cybersecurity field.

In summary, **staying updated on cybersecurity trends and threats** is a proactive commitment that requires ongoing learning, engagement, and adaptation. **Monitoring emerging cyber threats** through trusted news sources, social media, and expert analyses enables individuals and businesses to stay aware of the latest risks. Pursuing **continuing education and resources**, such as certifications and training programs, builds and reinforces essential cybersecurity skills.

Finally, **community engagement and support** from online forums, government resources, and industry events provide additional insights, practical advice, and encouragement, making it easier to keep up with the fast-paced world of cybersecurity. By embracing these strategies, individuals and businesses alike can maintain a robust defense against cyber threats and adapt to the evolving digital landscape with confidence.

Appendices and Resources

The **Appendices and Resources** section offers readers additional support, guidance, and reference materials to reinforce the concepts covered throughout this book. With a mix of definitions, checklists, templates, and useful contacts, this section provides practical tools for ongoing cybersecurity efforts and promotes a proactive approach to digital safety. Designed for easy reference, these resources are intended to simplify cybersecurity practices for individuals and small businesses, ensuring they have the essentials at their fingertips.

Glossary of Key Terms is a comprehensive list of definitions that clarify technical jargon and cybersecurity terminology used throughout the book. Understanding these terms is critical for building familiarity with cybersecurity concepts, and this glossary serves as a quick reference guide for readers. Here are a few examples of terms included:

- **Malware**: Software designed to harm, exploit, or otherwise compromise the functionality of a system. Examples include viruses, ransomware, and spyware.
- **Phishing**: A technique where attackers impersonate legitimate entities to trick individuals into revealing personal information, often through email or messages.
- **Encryption**: The process of converting data into a code to prevent unauthorized access. Encryption is commonly used to protect sensitive information.
- **Firewall**: A security system that monitors and controls incoming and outgoing network traffic, creating a barrier between trusted and untrusted networks.

- **Multi-Factor Authentication (MFA):** A security feature that requires users to verify their identity through multiple forms of verification, such as a password and a one-time code.
- **Ransomware:** A type of malware that encrypts files and demands payment (often in cryptocurrency) for their release.
- **Data Breach:** An incident where unauthorized individuals access sensitive or confidential information.
- **VPN (Virtual Private Network):** A tool that encrypts internet connections, providing a secure tunnel for online activity and protecting privacy.

This glossary empowers readers to build a foundational understanding of cybersecurity vocabulary, making it easier to engage with more advanced topics over time.

Checklists and Guides provide actionable steps for implementing specific security measures. These checklists help readers translate knowledge into practice, offering straightforward instructions for securing social media, configuring networks, and handling incidents.

Social Media Security Checklist is designed to protect personal and professional social media accounts. By following these steps, users can safeguard their profiles, limit data exposure, and reduce the risk of unauthorized access:

- **Set up a strong, unique password** for each social media account and enable multi-factor authentication (MFA).
- **Adjust privacy settings** to control who can view posts, friend lists, and personal information.

- **Review and limit third-party app permissions** connected to social media accounts to reduce exposure to external risks.
- **Be cautious with friend requests and messages** from unknown sources, as these may be phishing attempts or social engineering tactics.
- **Avoid oversharing personal information**, such as location and travel plans, to protect against physical and digital risks.
- **Regularly review activity logs** to detect any unusual login attempts or account changes.

Network Configuration Checklist offers guidelines for setting up secure home networks, an essential step for protecting connected devices from unauthorized access:

- **Change the default router username and password** to a strong, unique combination.
- **Enable WPA3 encryption** (or WPA2 if WPA3 is not available) to secure wireless connections.
- **Disable WPS (Wi-Fi Protected Setup)**, which can be vulnerable to brute-force attacks.
- **Set up a firewall** if the router supports it, and consider using additional firewall software for added security.
- **Regularly update the router firmware** to ensure any vulnerabilities are patched.
- **Create a guest network** for visitors, keeping it separate from the main network used for personal devices.
- **Disable remote management features** unless they are essential, as they can expose the network to external access.

Incident Response Template is a simple form to document cybersecurity incidents and responses. Accurate documentation is essential for evaluating the scope of an attack, identifying vulnerabilities, and refining future responses. This template provides a structured way to capture details:

- **Date and Time of Incident:** Document when the suspicious activity was first noticed.
- **Type of Incident:** Specify whether it was a phishing attack, malware infection, data breach, or another type.
- **Affected Systems and Data:** Note which devices, accounts, or data were compromised or targeted.
- **Immediate Actions Taken:** List steps taken to contain the attack, such as disconnecting devices or notifying IT support.
- **Notification and Communication:** Record who was informed about the

incident, including relevant staff, customers, or regulatory bodies.

- **Investigation Summary**: Describe any findings from security scans, forensic analysis, or logs.
- **Follow-up Measures**: Document improvements or changes made to prevent future incidents, such as updating software or refining policies.

Useful Contacts and Resources offer further support for ongoing cybersecurity needs, connecting readers to agencies, hotlines, and learning platforms.

Cybersecurity Hotlines and Agencies provide assistance and reporting options for individuals and small businesses facing cyber incidents. Knowing where to report incidents can facilitate a timely response and, in some cases, assist with recovery:

- **Cybersecurity and Infrastructure Security Agency (CISA)**: Offers

guidance on responding to cybersecurity incidents, including threat alerts and resources.
- **Federal Trade Commission (FTC)**: Assists with reporting identity theft, scams, and fraud, with resources for managing the impact.
- **Internet Crime Complaint Center (IC3)**: A division of the FBI, IC3 provides a platform for reporting cybercrimes, including fraud and hacking.
- **National Cyber Security Centre (NCSC)** (UK): Offers threat advisories, incident response guidelines, and cybersecurity support for businesses and the public.
- **Consumer Financial Protection Bureau (CFPB)**: Provides resources for reporting financial fraud and recovering from scams that impact credit or finances.

Further Reading suggests books, websites, and resources for those who wish to deepen their understanding of cybersecurity. These materials cover a range of topics, from technical guides to beginner-friendly explanations, making it easier for readers to expand their knowledge at their own pace:

- **Books**: "Cybersecurity for Dummies" by Joseph Steinberg provides a user-friendly introduction, while "The Art of Invisibility" by Kevin Mitnick offers insights into privacy and security techniques.
- **Websites**: Websites like **Cyber Aware** (from the UK government) and **StaySafeOnline.org** (powered by the National Cybersecurity Alliance) provide guides and tools for safe online practices.
- **Online Courses**: Platforms like **Coursera**, **edX**, and **Udemy** offer cybersecurity courses on a wide range of

topics, including introductory courses and advanced certifications.

- **Cybersecurity Blogs**: Sites like **Krebs on Security** and **Threatpost** provide timely news, alerts, and expert analysis on the latest cybersecurity issues.
- **Government Resources**: Many government websites offer free resources tailored to small businesses and individuals, such as the **NIST Cybersecurity Framework**, which is a useful reference for building security protocols.

In summary, the **Appendices and Resources** section equips readers with tools and guidance to put cybersecurity knowledge into action. A **Glossary of Key Terms** clarifies essential vocabulary, while **Checklists and Guides** provide actionable steps for social media security, network configuration, and incident documentation.

Useful Contacts and Resources connect readers to reporting agencies, additional learning materials, and community support, enabling them to continue growing their cybersecurity knowledge. These resources form a lasting foundation, empowering readers to confidently manage their cybersecurity needs in an ever-evolving digital world.

Conclusion

Throughout this guide, we have explored various aspects of cybersecurity, from understanding common threats and securing personal devices to creating recovery plans and staying informed about emerging risks. Each chapter builds on the idea that cybersecurity is not a single task but an ongoing commitment that requires consistent attention and adaptation. For individuals, this means adopting daily habits that protect personal data, such as creating strong passwords, enabling multi-factor authentication, and staying vigilant against phishing attempts.

For small businesses, it involves implementing structured policies, educating employees, and maintaining secure networks to protect sensitive customer and company information.

Cybersecurity is often viewed as a complex field, one that requires technical expertise and significant resources.

However, the truth is that anyone can take meaningful steps to enhance their digital security. By following simple yet effective practices—such as updating software regularly, backing up data, and being cautious about online interactions—anyone can strengthen their defenses and reduce their vulnerability to attacks. The goal is not to achieve absolute security but to create an environment that discourages attackers, reduces risks, and enables quick recovery if a breach does occur.

Recap the Importance of Proactive Security and Resilience because these qualities are the foundation of a secure digital life. Cyber threats evolve quickly, and attackers are constantly adapting their tactics to exploit new vulnerabilities. Staying a step ahead requires vigilance and a willingness to adjust strategies as needed.

Being proactive about cybersecurity doesn't mean living in fear; rather, it's about establishing habits and safeguards that allow for safe, confident interactions with technology. Building resilience means that even if an attack does happen, individuals and organizations can respond effectively, minimize damage, and recover swiftly.

Resilience in cybersecurity also comes from learning from past incidents. A successful cybersecurity strategy is not just about prevention but about preparation and response. Each chapter has provided practical advice on preparing for potential threats, from recognizing early warning signs to documenting incidents and improving systems based on past experiences. By regularly evaluating and refining security measures, individuals and organizations create a cycle of improvement, continuously strengthening their digital environments against new and evolving threats.

Resilience transforms cybersecurity from a defensive measure to a proactive approach that promotes growth, learning, and adaptability.

The journey to digital security is ongoing, and this guide serves as a starting point, encouraging readers to adopt habits that will support their safety over the long term. Every action taken to secure one's digital life—whether it's enabling privacy settings on social media, setting up secure networks at home, or training employees in cybersecurity awareness—adds to a layered defense that is harder to penetrate. The more layers of security in place, the less likely an individual or organization is to become a target. This layered approach to cybersecurity is accessible, adaptable, and empowers users to protect their digital spaces with confidence.

Encourage Continued Learning and Staying Vigilant in the Digital Age because the world of cybersecurity is always changing.

Cyber threats evolve, and attackers continuously develop new methods for exploiting systems and people. As technology advances, so do the risks, which means that maintaining security requires constant vigilance and a commitment to learning. Continued education, awareness, and adaptation are the keys to staying safe in this dynamic environment.

This book has covered many core concepts and actionable steps, but cybersecurity is a vast field with new developments emerging regularly. By staying informed—through cybersecurity blogs, news sources, or even government alerts—readers can keep pace with the latest threats and adjust their defenses as needed. Learning doesn't stop here; it is an ongoing process that keeps individuals and businesses prepared to face the unknowns of the digital world.

Small businesses, in particular, benefit greatly from staying current on cybersecurity trends, as this enables them to protect their operations, employees, and customers more effectively. Individuals can do the same on a personal level, protecting themselves, their families, and their personal information.

One of the most empowering steps a reader can take is to view cybersecurity as a shared responsibility. Engaging with others about cybersecurity, whether it's discussing safe practices with family members, sharing security tips with coworkers, or joining online cybersecurity communities, helps build a culture of awareness and protection. Security is strongest when everyone takes part, contributing to an environment where awareness and caution are the norm. By encouraging others to follow cybersecurity best practices, readers can help protect not only their immediate circle but also contribute to a safer digital community overall.

The resources listed in the Appendices and Resources section offer numerous pathways for continued learning. Certifications, courses, and online forums provide opportunities for deeper engagement with cybersecurity topics, allowing individuals to expand their skills and knowledge as they become more familiar with the field.

For those interested in advanced topics or careers in cybersecurity, these resources serve as valuable starting points. However, even those with no professional interest in cybersecurity can benefit from regular updates and guidance from trusted sources. Cybersecurity awareness doesn't have to be time-consuming or technical—it can be as simple as reading a monthly newsletter or following industry leaders on social media.

In conclusion, cybersecurity is an essential part of modern life. By taking proactive steps, building resilience, and committing to continuous learning, individuals and organizations can navigate the digital world safely.

This book has provided a roadmap to help readers secure their digital lives, offering practical tools and insights for tackling the complex world of cybersecurity. The journey doesn't end here; rather, it's a stepping stone toward ongoing awareness, improvement, and empowerment. By staying vigilant, informed, and proactive, readers can protect themselves, their families, and their businesses in a world that grows more interconnected each day.

The power to create a secure digital life lies in your hands. Embrace the knowledge, use the tools, and continue learning to keep your defenses strong. Cybersecurity may be challenging, but it is achievable, and each step taken toward it is a step toward greater control, safety, and peace of mind in the digital age.

www.ingramcontent.com/pod-product-compliance
Lightning Source LLC
Chambersburg PA
CBHW071515220526
45472CB00003B/1035